The Soul's Sonata

Sai Kripa Karthikeyan

BookLeaf Publishing

India | USA | UK

Presentation by *BookLeaf Publishing*

Web: www.bookleafpub.com

E-mail: info@bookleafpub.com

ISBN: 9789360947514

First edition 2024

DEDICATION

To all those who dare to dream, who find solace in the beauty of words, and who believe in the power of the human spirit to transcend boundaries and reach for the stars. This book is dedicated to you, the dreamers, the seekers, and the believers. May the verses within these pages ignite your imagination, stir your soul, and remind you that within each of us lies the capacity for greatness.

Your Soulful Wordsmith,

Sai Kripa K

ACKNOWLEDGEMENT

In the grand symphony of life, there are countless melodies that intertwine to create a harmonious chorus. To each note in this beautiful composition, I extend my heartfelt gratitude and appreciation.

To the vast cosmos, for inspiring me to wonder and awe at you, and for teaching me that you-the universe hold boundless possibilities and endless beauty.

To my Taekwondo master and coaches, thank you for guiding me on this sacred path. Your teachings transcend the dojo, instilling in me values of perseverance, respect, and resilience.

To the teachers who have shared their knowledge and wisdom, shaping my intellect and nurturing my curiosity, thank you for illuminating the pathways of learning and enlightenment.

To my beloved family and friends, whose unwavering love, support, and encouragement have been the linchpin of my journey. Your unwavering belief in me has been a constant source of strength and inspiration, and I am eternally grateful to have you as the steadfast pillars in the narrative of my life.

To the dedicated publishing team who have worked tirelessly to bring this book to life, thank you for your passion, professionalism, and commitment to excellence. Your dedication and expertise have transformed words into art, and I am deeply appreciative of your efforts.

To you, the most cherished companion on this literary odyssey, thank you for embarking on this journey with me. Your curiosity, empathy, and open-mindedness breathe life into these pages, and it is your connection to these words that give them meaning and purpose.

And finally, to all others who have played a part, whether seen or unseen, known or unknown, thank you for contributing your unique essence to the tapestry of my life. Together, we have woven a story of friendship, resilience, and the boundless potential of the human spirit.

PREFACE

As I hold the pen in my hand to write this preface for my book, "The Soul's Sonata," I am flooded with the countless moments in my life where I felt the presence of something greater than myself. A mysterious force, an intangible power, that has always seemed to guide me towards certain paths, people, and experiences that would eventually shape me into the person I am today. It's as if this force had an unfathomable understanding of my deepest desires, my greatest fears, and my most heartfelt aspirations, and it is this force that I call the 'Soul'.

For me, the soul is not just a concept or an abstract idea. It is a tangible presence that communicates with us through the signs, senses, songs, and symbols of the universe. It is the voice that whispers in our ears when we are lost, the hand that guides us through the darkness, and the light that illuminates our path.

Throughout my life, I have felt the soul's presence in countless ways. It has voiced to me through the beauty of nature, the rare opportunities, and the serendipitous events that seem to align perfectly to lead me towards my destiny. And it is this journey of discovery, of learning to listen to the soul's voice and follow its guidance, that has inspired the poems in this collection.

"The Soul's Sonata" is not just a collection of poems. It is a reflection of my life, a testament to the power of the soul, and a celebration of the beauty of the universe's symphony. Each poem is a piece of the larger puzzle, a note in the grand symphony of life that we are all a part of.

As you read these poems, I invite you to listen to the voice of your own soul, to pay attention to the signs and songs that the universe is sending your way, and to trust that the path you are on is leading you towards your own unique destiny. Because just as every note in a symphony is crucial to creating the whole, so too is your life important in creating the larger tapestry of the universe. So let these poems be a reminder that you are not alone on your journey. That the soul is with you always, guiding you towards your highest potential. And that the universe is speaking to you in every moment, if only you have the ears to hear.

My Cognomen

There is an adolescent,
There is a soul of curio.
There is a Mind of dreams,
There are questions roaming hither and yon,
Trying to find answers to what they say is
ludicrous.

Rabbit on through the fields of spherules,
Clearing the icy earthen in the lane,
Reconnoitering to yonder the precincts of the
heavens.
Igniting a red zeal down below,
To Find the story on a new orbiter like our own.
There is the nonpareil of everyone,
Here is the idiosyncratic 'SAI KRIPA'.

Grounded Flight

Oh, curiosity, you were once a bird!
Soaring high, to new heights, undeterred,
Through skies of knowledge, you flew with grace.
And the mysteries of the world were yours to embrace.

But now, in this modern world, your wings seem clipped,
As distractions and apathy leave you stripped,
The cages of technology, they seem to hold you tight.
And the wonder that once fueled you, has vanished from sight.

Where once you sang with joy, in the sun's warm
light,
Now you're confined to a world of endless night.
And the melodies that once flowed from your
beak,
Are now silenced, by the chaos of the modern
week.

Oh, curiosity, how some of us mourn your loss
For in this modern world, you're now just a cross
A symbol of what once was, but is now gone
A reminder of a spirit, that we've left alone

But we hold out hope, that someday you'll fly
That your wings will be freed, and you'll once
again try
To reach for the heavens, and embrace the new
To rediscover the world, and all that it can do

For you are not just a bird, but a symbol of hope
A reminder of the beauty, that's within our scope
And though the world may seem dark, and filled
with strife
We know that with your spirit, we can reclaim
life.

A Taekwondian's Heartbeat

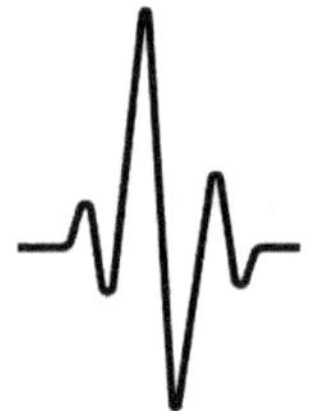

Taekwondo, oh Taekwondo,
My heart beats with this name,
A passion burning deep within,
A love that's not just a game.

The respect for the art I hold,
Is like no other can compare,
A discipline that molds the soul,
And makes me want to dare.

The power of a well-placed kick,
The grace of a flying jump,
The focus of a meditative mind,
All in Taekwondo I bump.

Years of training, sweat and tears,
Have made me strong and true,
I stand tall with my head held high,
A Taekwondian through and through.

For those who share my love and respect,
For the art that we hold dear,
We stand together, side by side,
With Taekwondo, we have no fear.

Connected By Stars

The night sky is a breathtaking sight,
A canvas painted with countless stars of light.
The Milky Way flows like a river divine,
Guiding our thoughts to places far and fine.
The silver moon, a beacon of grace,
Illuminates the world with its gentle face.
The city below, a cluster of light,
A tranquil haven in the midst of the night.
We're but a speck in the infinite space,
Yet we hold the power to light up this place.
United by the stars that twinkle above,
We're bound together by an unbreakable love.

Heart of a Storm

Amidst the raging storm of strife,
A heart that beats, a soul that's alive.
The winds of war may blow and churn,
But deep within, a fire still burns.

Like a ship that sails upon the seas,
The calm amidst the storm brings peace.
The tempest rages, the waves grow tall,
But the ship stays steady, standing tall.

In this war-torn world, a calm does dwell,
A place where hope and love do swell.
Where even in the darkest night,
A spark of light can shine so bright.

The battlefield may rage and roar,
But the calm within can still restore.
A heart that's pure, a soul that's free,
Can rise above the stormy sea.

So let us find that calm within,
And let it guide us through the din.
For amid war's cruel fate,
The calm can help us navigate.

Moments You Weave

Life is a tapestry of memories,
Woven by the moments we create,
So, cherish each moment, make it count,
And revel in the joy it brings.

When the darkness looms and troubles you,
Remember that life is beautiful,
It's the little moments that make it so,
And they're worth all the struggles you go
through.

Make each moment a masterpiece,
A work of art that's truly unique,
And when you look back on your life,
You'll see a canvas that's rich and complete.

So, let your love light shine,
And share your moments with those who matter,
For they are the ones who make life worth
living,
And who fill it with love, joy, and laughter.

Curiosity's Canvas

In the garden of numbers, let's take a stroll,
Where mysteries abound, and wonders enroll.
Mathematics, a canvas of infinite hue,
A tapestry of possibilities, ever anew.

Like a river that flows, through valleys and
glades,
Mathematics meanders, through unseen
cascades.
With curiosity as our compass, we embark,
To unlock its secrets, in the light and the dark.

Fear not the unknown, for in every fold,
Lies a treasure untold, waiting to be told.
Just as a seed in the soil, yearns to grow,
Mathematics beckons, with a gentle glow.

It's not about knowing, but daring to see,
The beauty it holds, in its complexity.
Like a prism of light, it refracts and reframes,
Revealing connections, where once were just
names.

So let's embrace this journey, with open hearts
wide,
For in the realm of mathematics, there's nothing
to hide.
With curiosity as our guide, we'll soar and we'll
fly,
And find that within us, the numbers don't lie.

For in every equation, and theorem we find,
Lies a story untold, of the curious mind.
So fear not, for in mathematics' embrace,
We'll discover a world, where all find their
place.

Paradoxical Elegance

In the realm of words where poetry reigns,
There dwells a creature, beauty unchained.
With flowing robes of metaphor and rhyme,
She dances gracefully through the sands of time.

Her voice, a melody of syllables sweet,
In every stanza, she finds her beat.
With irony's twist, she weaves her tale,
In paradoxes, her whispers prevail.

She strolls through forests of simile's bloom,
Under moonlit skies where metaphors loom.
In the garden of verse, she tends to each line,
Nurturing beauty, oh so divine.

Yet, irony dances within her embrace,
In jest and contradiction, she finds her space.
For what is beauty without a touch of the
strange,
A paradoxical truth, a poetic exchange?

She paints with hues of paradox's charm,
Crafting sonnets that disarm.
In the irony of life, her essence unfurls,
A paradoxical gem in the kingdom of pearls.

So raise your pens to this creature so rare,
Whose beauty lies in her ironic flair.
For in the heart of every poem, she gleams,
A paradoxical symphony of dreams.

Echoes of Error

In the hum of circuits, I find my way,
Lost in the realm of a digital day.
A modern world, where screens reign supreme,
Yet within its grip, I drift and dream.

As I code and craft with clicks and taps,
A glitch appears, disrupting the maps.
But before I can delve into the fray,
The machine corrects, guiding my way.

In the shadow of algorithms grand,
I feel a longing for a distant land.
Where errors were teachers, lessons in disguise,
And wisdom bloomed beneath clearer skies.

For in this world of instant correction,
I ache for the beauty of imperfection,
Where each flaw was a chance to grow,
And every setback helped us to know.

But now, in the glow of screens so bright,
Mistakes vanish in the blink of light.
And though progress marches, swift and sure,
I yearn for the struggles that made us endure.
For in the heart of each error found,
Lies the essence of wisdom, profound.
A journey of discovery, a path we tread,
Where lessons learned are never misled.

So let me embrace this nostalgic plea,
For the errors that once shaped me.
In a world of technology's allure,
I'll cherish the lessons, timeless and pure.

Die Laughing

In the dark of night, beneath the moon's soft
glow,
Stands a man, brave, with courage aglow.
Amid chaos, amidst the strife,
He laughs at death, embracing life.

Through battles fierce, and bullets whizzing by,
He stands tall, with a fearless eye.
Though he may own the wealth of torpedoes,
He lacks the wisdom of fear, resisting the
supremacy,
His laughter echoing across the battlefield.

With every step he takes, he defies the odds,
Laughing in the face of death, against all gods.
His laughter, a beacon amidst the despair,
A testament to the strength he bears.

For in the heart of war, where danger reigns,
He finds solace in laughter, amidst the pains.
For in laughter's embrace, he finds his might,
A soldier unyielding in the darkest night.

So let the cannons roar, let the enemies jeer.
For the soldier's laughter shall wipe all fear.
In the face of death, he stands tall and free,
For in laughter's echo, he finds victory.

Unique Earthlings

Oh Dear Earthlings!!
At Mars, you glance at the powder of dust,
Vast and red, with ghastly winds and hindering
space to breathe.
At Venus you barely sniff, you better spare an
umbrella,
To manage yourself through the pain from the
thundershower on this telluric planet.

Back on Earth life is like a utopia of delight!!!
But back in a million years, this Paradise was a
pandemonium.
Every side, every second a volcano collapses,
Later, there was an era of shiver,
The earthly sphere was crystal-clear as a wall of
silver.

Just then was the period of Life,
Little shoots sprouted, ice just rendered, and
interphase began.
One by one, and Two by Two life thrived,
And then came Brainy EARTHLINGS.

Established the Pandemonium, the Best Place, to
continue life.
Oh Dear EARTHLINGS!!! Oh Dear
EARTHLINGS,
You have a heart of passion, thoughts of
curiosity
You created tools; You created the new Epic
World of Peace,
You care for the eco-system; You care for the
universe.
And you are busy...… And you are busy.…
searching for friends in stellar space.

Symphony Of Life

In the stillness of the chapel's embrace,
Where tears fall like raindrops, serene,
Nature weaves its tapestry profound,
With beauty in every sight and sound.

As rhythmic teardrops meet the earth,
Like gentle rain in a dance of rebirth,
They mingle with petals, soft and fair,
A fragrant symphony fills the air.

The fragrance of flowers, a sweet embrace,
Amidst the sorrow, a touch of grace,
Each bloom a whisper of life's fleeting art,
In the garden of grief, they play their part.

While mourners weep, the world moves on,
In the meadows, the rivers, at dawn,
The sun still rises, the birds still sing,
Life's eternal rhythm, an endless spring.

In the rustle of leaves, a gentle sigh,
As branches sway 'neath the azure sky,
Nature's whispers echo, soft and wise,
A reminder that beauty never dies.

For in the cycle of life and death,
There's beauty found in every breath,
In the tears that fall, the flowers' bloom,
Nature's symphony fills the room.

So let the tears and raindrops fall,
As nature weeps and hearts recall,
For in the mourning's tender grace,
There lies a beauty in the final embrace.

The Urgent Detergent

In the bustling city, where seriousness thrives,

Lived a man named Sam, with serious vibes.

With a suit so sharp and a face so stern,

He took everything seriously, to learn.

From meetings to memos, he had no time for
play,

Seriousness was his mantra, come what may.

He'd frown at a joke, scoff at a jest,

To him, laughter was a dubious test.

But one fine day, in his office so grand,

Sam found himself in a prankster's hand.

For while typing away, with a furrowed brow,

He accidentally sent an email, oh wow!

The email, you see, was meant to be stern,

But a typo transformed it, to Sam's concern.

Instead of "urgent," it read "detergent",

A mishap that set off a comedic version.

The email went out, to the entire team,

And laughter erupted, like a bubbling stream.

For Sam had unwittingly made a joke,

And now he found himself in quite a poke.

The office roared with laughter, at Sam's
expense,

As he tried to salvage his serious pretense.

But the more he tried, the funnier it got,

And soon Sam found himself in quite a spot.

For even the most serious of souls,

Can't escape the humor that life unfolds.

And though Sam's face remained stoic and stern,

Inside he was laughing, a lesson to learn.

So here's to Sam, the serious guy,

Who fell for a prank, without a sly.

Harmony of Strategy

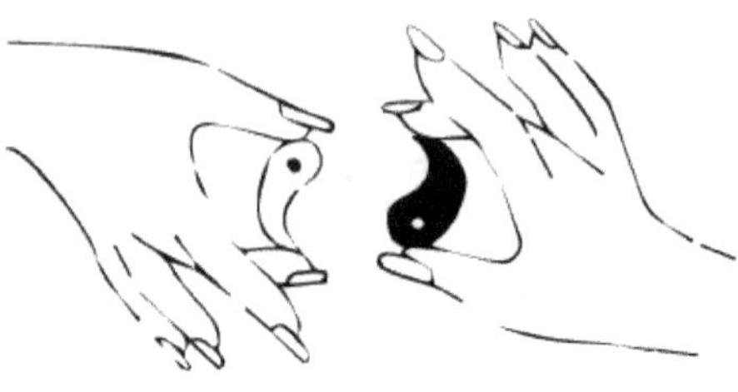

In the arena of life, two realms unfold,
Where tales of mastery and cunning are told.
One is the dance of feet in the air,
The other a battle of intellect laid bare.

Taekwondo, a symphony of motion and might,
Where warriors spar in the arena's bright light.
With kicks that soar like arrows in flight,
Each movement a step towards victory's height.

Chess, the silent battlefield of the mind,
Where strategists plot, their tactics refined.
With every move, a web of plans entwined,
Each piece a pawn in the grand design.

In Taekwondo's bout, opponents engage,
With precision and skill, they write their page.
Each strike a move on life's vibrant stage,
In the rhythm of combat, they find their gauge.

In chess's board, the pieces stand tall,
Each one a player in the mind's grand hall.
Bishops, knights, and queens, they all enthrall,
In the game of intellect, where minds enthrall.

Yet beneath the surface, they share a kin,
In the art of strategy, where battles begin.
For in Taekwondo and chess, we see within,
The essence of mastery, where victories win.

Both are games of patience and finesse,
Where tactics and timing can bring success.
In the dance of combat or the mind's chess,
The masters find glory, no more, no less.

Our Furry Friend

In a cozy home, where friendships bloom,

There dwells a furry friend, dispelling gloom.

With eyes that sparkle, a heart so pure too,

Lives a pup named Miles, with fluffy gains.

As I step inside, he greets me with glee,

A joyful "woof" and a wagging spree.

Panting with excitement, tail in the air,

Miles fills the room with love and care.

But it's those eyes, oh how they gleam,

As Miles stares deeply, like in a dream.

At the table, as we gather round,

He casts his spell, he steals our hearts,

With pleading eyes, he knows so well.
So we share our food, to his delight.

With each gentle pat on his silky fur,

Miles wags his tail, a contented purr.

In the midst of play, he's a bundle of joy,

Jumping and catching, his favorite toy.

With boundless energy, he fills the air,

Bringing laughter and smiles, without a care.

So here's to Miles, our dear furry friend,

Whose love and loyalty will never end.

In his playful antics, we find delight,

A cherished companion, shining bright.

Romance with Words

In the quiet sanctuary of my mind's domain,
Books are windows, each page a lane.
I journey through realms, both near and far,
Lost in the dance of a writer's memoir.

Each word a brushstroke on life's canvas bright,
Painting scenes of wonder, of depth, of light.
In the tapestry of tales, I find my delight,
A symphony of stories, ever in flight.

Writing, a dance of heart and pen,
Ink flowing freely, where thoughts begin.
Each line a melody, each stanza a song,
In the universe of words, I belong.

With every turn of the page, I soar,
Exploring worlds never seen before.
In the rhythm of reading, I find my peace,
A refuge, a haven, where worries cease.

So let me linger in this love divine,
In the magic of prose, in the verse's line.
For in the world of books and poems dear,
I find my solace, my joy, my cheer.

Beneath the Silent Skies

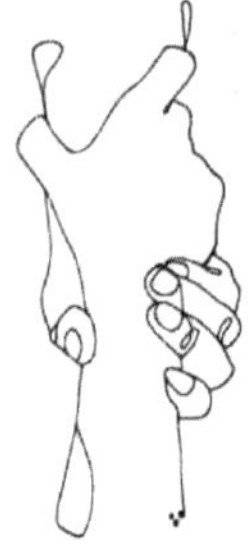

In the realm where shadows dance,
Amidst the echoes of fate's trance,
A silent light, a beacon bright,
Guiding me through the darkest night.

Not just a voice, but a whispered hymn,
A symphony of wisdom in the dim.
In the crucible of challenge and flame,
He emerges, not by title, but by name.

A brother forged in the furnace of time,
His presence, a rhythm, a subtle chime.
Through trials and triumphs, he stands tall,
A steadfast pillar amidst the squall.

His words, like arrows, sharp and true,
Pierce through doubt, unveiling the view.
In his gaze, a depth untold,
A reservoir of stories, ancient and bold.

Though our words may be few and far between,
In the silence, a bond unseen.
For he knows my spirit, my deepest fears,
And in his presence, they disappear.

Harsh and stern, yet tender and kind,
A paradox of the human mind.
For his scolds, a refining fire,
Forging strength from my deepest desire.

In the stadium of life, he's my trusted guide,
So in the quiet moments, when shadows fall,
I know I can trust him, hear his call.
With each step, his wisdom imparts,
Whose light guides me until the very end.

Stellar Bond

In the vast expanse where the ocean roars,
I sailed, not seeking, just drifting ashore.
Amidst the waves, in the celestial dome,
A lone star beckoned, guiding me home.

A chance encounter, a cosmic dance,
As if fate whispered, giving chance a chance.
This star, in the sky's embrace,
With a light so pure, a radiant grace.

We're akin, like stars in constellations,
Yet distinct in our own unique manifestations.
Together we navigate life's vast sea,
Bound by a thread of destiny.

In the ocean of existence, turmoil and strife,
We found solace in each other's light,
True and loyal, through ebb and flow,
Our bond, like stars, continues to glow.

But in the heavens, amidst the gleam,
Betrayal lurks, a treacherous scheme.
Stars flicker and fade, their light astray,
Yet ours burns bright, come what may.

For we, like stars, defy the night,
Guiding each other with unwavering light,
In a sky crowded with false allure.

Love to the power of Infinity

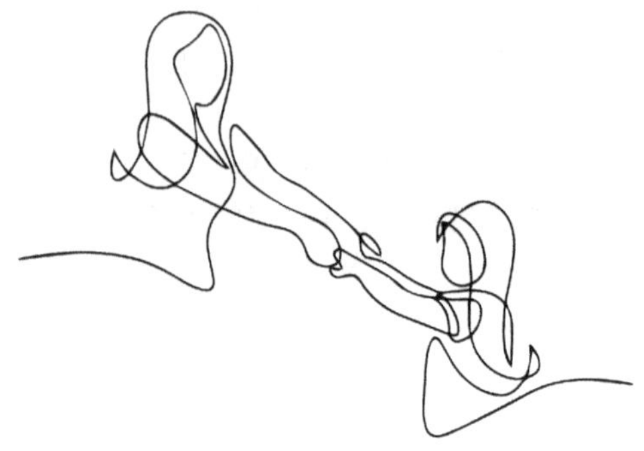

In the cradle of her love, I find my solace,
A mother's touch, a boundless grace.
Though her words may sting, like lashes in the
wind,
Her love, a fortress, in which I'm pinned.

A teacher of the ledgers, a lecturer of dreams,
She sacrificed it all, or so it seems.
Her dreams she placed upon the shelf,
To nurture mine, with boundless wealth.

In her eyes, I see the stars align,
A universe of love, endlessly divine.
Though her path diverged, from dreams once
held dear,
Her love, unwavering, ever sincere.

Through storms of anger, and seas of regret,
Her love, a lighthouse, I'll never forget.
For in her heart, a melody sings,
Of sacrifice, and the joy it brings.

In her hands, she crafts beauty untold,
A tapestry of love, in fashion's hold.
With creativity as her guiding light,
She weaves dreams in the darkest night.

I may stumble, and I may fall,
But in her love, I find my all.
For she is more than a mother, more than a
friend,
She is my world, without the end.

So though the winds of anger may blow,
In her love, I find my truest glow.
For her love knows no bounds, no end in sight,
A beacon of hope, in love's eternal light.

My First Sensei

In the shadows of dawn, where dreams take
flight,
Stands a titan of strength, a beacon of light.
With fists of wisdom, and a heart of gold,
My father, my hero, courageous and bold.

In the dojo of life, he's a master of grace,
Guiding me through each challenging race.
With the spirit of Bruce Lee, he inspires me
high,
To conquer my fears, to reach for the sky.

In the hustle of life, amidst calls that chime,
He finds time for me, every single time.
Skipping meals, his sacrifice profound,
To ensure my happiness, my dreams unbound.

A warrior of work, relentless and strong,
Yet in his eyes, I see where I belong.
For he believes in my every endeavor,
Fueling my spirit with boundless fervor.

In the realm of sports, he's my biggest fan,
Cheering me on, with a proud, loving stand.
With every punch, every kick, every throw,
His love and support, like a steady flow.

A visionary thinker, future's embrace,
In his mind, innovation finds its place.
If he were an inventor, his brilliance would
shine,
Inventing a world where love intertwines.

With every workout, he teaches me well,
That health is wealth, a story to tell.
For in his strength, I find my might,
A bond unbroken, shining bright.

So here's to my father, my rock, my guide,
In his love and wisdom, I forever abide.
For he's not just a man, but my superhero,
In his embrace, I find my truest zero.

Knitting the Horizons

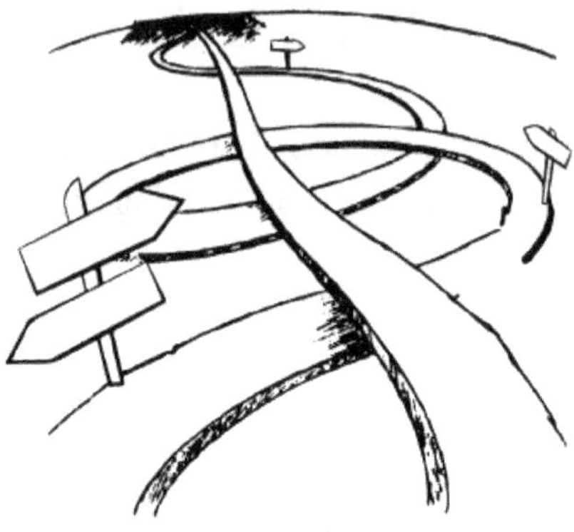

In the realm of dreams, where aspirations soar,
I walk a path, uncertain, yet longing for more.
A lover of learning, a fighter in the ring,
I strive to prove the harmony these passions
bring.

In the echoes of doubt, whispers fill the air,
That to excel in both, one must choose and pare.
But I refuse to accept such limiting views,
For in my heart, the connection I refuse to lose.

Taekwondo, a dance of strength and grace,
Space, a journey to the stars' embrace.
In each, a quest for mastery and light,
Yet society's barriers obscure the sight.

I yearn to bridge the gap, to break the mold,
To show the world the truth, bold and bold.
For in the discipline of the mind, and the spirit's
flight,
Lies the essence of greatness, burning bright.

Cosmos calls to me, with its mysteries untold,
While Taekwondo ignites my spirit, strong and
bold.
Why must I choose between the two, when both
ignite my soul?
I refuse to surrender, to let limitations take their
toll.

For in the arena of life, where battles are won,
I'll stand as proof that both can be done.
With dedication and perseverance, I'll show the
way,
That sports and education are intertwined, come
what may.

So let the doubters speak their words of scorn,
I'll rise above, my spirit unshorn.
For in the fusion of mind and body, I'll find my
grace,
And in the pursuit of knowledge, I'll find my
place.

Though the journey be long, and the road
unclear,
I'll walk with courage, banishing fear.
For I am the bridge between worlds, shining
bright,
Proving that sports and education always unite.